BRIGHT SHADE

WINNERS OF THE AMERICAN POETRY REVIEW/ HONICKMAN FIRST BOOK PRIZE

1998   Joshua Beckman, *Things Are Happening*

1999   Dana Levin, *In the Surgical Theatre*

2000   Anne Marie Macari, *Ivory Cradle*

2001   Ed Pavlić, *Paraph of Bone & Other Kinds of Blue*

2002   Kathleen Ossip, *The Search Engine*

2003   James McCorkle, *Evidences*

2004   Kevin Ducey, *Rhinoceros*

2005   Geoff Bouvier, *Living Room*

2006   David Roderick, *Blue Colonial*

2007   Gregory Pardlo, *Totem*

2008   Matthew Dickman, *All-American Poem*

2009   Laura McKee, *Uttermost Paradise Place*

2010   Melissa Stein, *Rough Honey*

2011   Nathaniel Perry, *Nine Acres*

2012   Tomás Q. Morín, *A Larger Country*

2013   Maria Hummel, *House & Fire*

2014   Katherine Bode-Lang, *The Reformation*

2015   Alicia Jo Rabins, *Divinity School*

2016   Heather Tone, *Likenesses*

2017   Tyree Daye, *River Hymns*

2018   Jacob Saenz, *Throwing the Crown*

2019   Taneum Bambrick, *Vantage*

2020   Chessy Normile, *Great Exodus, Great Wall, Great Party*

2021   Natasha Rao, *Latitude*

Bright Shade

Chelsea Harlan

The American Poetry Review
Philadelphia

For Buck — my old friend, my speckled shepherd.

Cover art is "Giovanna" by Nate Luce. Glass beads and wax on masonite, artist's concrete frame, 2018. (Photo by Henry Austin) Book design and composition: Gopa & Ted 2, Inc.

Distribution by Copper Canyon Press/Consortium

Library of Congress Control Number: 2022939980

ISBN 978-0-9860938-5-2 (cloth, alk. paper)
ISBN 978-0-9860938-6-9 (pbk., alk. paper)

98765432 FIRST EDITION

CONTENTS

Introduction by Jericho Brown   1

one

Nature Documentary   9
The Big Egg   10
Bright Angel   11
In the Rearview   12
Love Poem Called Die Hard   14
Here and There   15
Still Time All Day   17
Poem for a Fern   18
Mama Recites the Birds   19

two

Bobby Boris Pickett   23
It's Sunday so We Get High by the River   24
I Went for a Long Ride   25
Sonnet Near Zyzzyx   26
Adidas   27
Plain Air   29
Two Pilgrims   30
Things We've Thrown   31
Mama Recites the Trees   32
Miracle-Gro   36

three

Career   39
Some Sunlight   40
Beautiful Daggers   41
Homecoming Pain   42

Sweet Pea   43

Jenny Talking about Twilight Knowing   44

Future Brooches   45

Late Spring Poem   46

Leaving the House   50

four

Summer of the Wild Boars   53

The Long Blue Dress   54

Mama Sows the Ginseng Seeds   56

Romance Language   57

Sonnet for a Good Cry in the Woods   60

Nightgown   61

I Have Yet More Esotericism to Share   62

True Life: 63

five

Grimaldo's Chair   67

The Little News   68

He Loves Me   69

The Fleece   70

Poem for a Fieldmouse   72

My Neighbor Says His Friend Says   73

Mama Recites the Horses   74

Alone Time   77

Sonnet from Last July   79

six

Drama Club   83

Another Sunday Poem   84

The Birds Did It   86

Aimlessness   87

Sonnet for Your Soils   88

This Is Also That   89

Mama Recites the Plot of a
Liam Neeson Movie Called Honest Thief   90
After Hours   91
Livepower, or, Biodynamism   94
Benediction   95
Resolutions   97

Notes   98
Acknowledgments   100

INTRODUCTION
by Jericho Brown

CHELSEA HARLAN's *Bright Shade* begins with two epigraphs: one from the late great poet C.D. Wright, known for her documentary poetics of ethics and innovation, and another from singer-songwriter Roger Miller, known for whimsical lyrics that made his music perfect for children watching the Disney animated film *Robin Hood*. These two influences are apt introductions to a book that honors the value of and enacts the fact of real, human delight, a subject and feeling there may not be enough of in contemporary American poetry.

Harlan's poems' chief concern is pleasure. Her speakers seem to long for it or to be luxuriating in it: "The cats do this thing where they sleep/all day in America waiting to be loved." And one of the world's greatest pleasures is the pleasure of poetry itself. Therefore, Harlan's poems always turn and surprise and leap. Her diction shifts several times in a single line, and yet, each line in any poem depends on one another:

> "Woof, mindfulness is exhausting
> but the thing is it's so ineffable
> it's resistant to irony
>
> Mindfulness doesn't give a fuck
> about what you think about mindfulness
> That's the beauty of it, I say
>
> The moon sure is full of itself
> Do you ever see a rabbit in it
> churning some butter, or
>
> Mindfulness's indifferent, like the wind
> That's beautiful, he says thoughtfully
> and carefully all falls still in the yard

Thank you, I reply walleyed,
I put it in a romantic poem
I put the moon in most passwords"

Often these poems make their impact by way of list or litany, and
while they are chiefly written in free verse, they depend on rhyme
and meter in ways that show the poet's understanding of the genre's
history and how to craft a new contribution as that history continues:

"Our server said his name was Derrick
and that he'd be our server tonight and
Derrick doesn't care about the view anymore
He said you get used to it after awhile
He said people like to freak out about the elk
And I thought people like to freak out in general
thus Black Friday and horror as an escapism genre
and Elmo and the World Cup and royal weddings
and especially solar eclipses for their rarity
Something to do with adrenaline, spectacle
Not to be confused with real, high-stakes fear
You ordered a brownie and ice cream to go
You left the ice cream outside on the porch
in the cold to keep it cold in the snow"

These lyric love poems become all the more convincing when their
humor and whimsy gets grounded in geographic place and what
seems documented fact. The whole of this book reads like a wild road
trip two lovers take at the last minute from the East Coast to the West
Coast and back again. But this couple always finds themselves rooted
to the land no matter where they travel, and many of their discoveries
are those of people who farm and swim in the nearest lake and spend
time gazing at the moon:

"That small thunder thunders as I enter the barn
As the steer's legs fold beneath him like a card
His open eyes like out of order crystal balls

Like he was in the middle of delivering prophecy
Blood sneaks under the hay to the floor of the manger
That place of divine birth and of modest death
There's incarnation and then there's excarnation,
Stephen says, and that's just how it all goes
Thank you for helping me wash my hands
Thank you for lunch and the little bowl hit
And for going down on me despite everything
As if one of these days will really be the end"

Harlan shines brightest when she expands that love of the land to include her mother's and aunt's love for it. I fell in love with this book and understood how serious it is about its tenderness when I came upon poems like "Mama Recites the Birds," "Mama Recites the Trees," and "Mama Sows the Ginseng Seeds." These first two relate what seems a real-life answer to questions posed to the mother by her daughter the poet. And in the answers, Harlan finds the lyric moment in ancestral vernacular and in misspoken English:

"Eddie who threw me numerous times
Threw me like three times

He was the one that got ruptured in his penis by Sam the pony

So Sam the pony and Liz
are buried here
in the very bottom below the patio"

But all of this always leads back to love of the land and a respect for it as if describing it is a ritual, a holy act. Here is "Mama Sows the Ginseng Seeds:"

"On the other side of the new creek
above bottle dump first plot between
rocks and cut walnut tree on the
fence line next other side of downed
tree base of poplar fourth plot near

under grape vine fifth plot upstream
across from old hunting stand past
double grape vine under poplar with
one grape vine locust behind it next
plot twenty feet above near fence
between double trunk tree and small
stones two on top of a larger one
twelve feet up next to fence next
one ten feet up planted five for the
sun stopped at rocks old stump with
wire next down and past old stump
planted five cross over walnut tree
planted in front of broken egg rock
day two lower field cross stream
and upstream just a bit from beech
tree field side in front of smaller
beech tree next across from bottom
field on fence line near downed pine
planted beside ironwood tree further
down on fence row in front of old
metal bucket past downed ash tree
in front and beside cedars way down
on the other side of the old creek"

But I should be clear and say that Chelsea Harlan is not a poet of experience as much as she is a poet who uses language to transform experience, a poet who understands the poem as its own experience. *Bright Shade* is always playful but in a way that asks the reader to join in with the play, to fully participate in a poetry that enjoys language enough to arrive at the most serious of realizations.

Jericho Brown
Atlanta

~

Melon, not cake, was served;
there was japonica and spirea. Still
they were a little late for the forsythia.
God yes, the forsythia, the forsythia.

— C.D. WRIGHT, from "Mountain Herald"

Robin Hood and Little John, walking through the forest
Laughing back and forth at what the other one has to say
Reminiscing this and that and having such a good time
Oo-de-lally, oo-de-lally, golly, what a day

Never ever thinking there was danger in the water
They were drinking, they just guzzled it down
Never dreaming that a scheming sheriff and his posse
Was a-watching them and gathering around

Robin Hood and Little John, running through the forest
Jumping fences, dodging trees, and trying to get away
Contemplating nothing but escape and finally making it
Oo-de-lally, oo-de-lally, golly, what a day

Oo-de-lally, oo-de-lally, golly, what a day

— ROGER MILLER, *Robin Hood*

one

Nature Documentary

The cats do this thing where they sleep
all day in America waiting to be loved

The Big Egg

Woof, mindfulness is exhausting
but the thing is it's so ineffable
it's resistant to irony

Mindfulness doesn't give a fuck
about what you think about mindfulness
That's the beauty of it, I say

The moon sure is full of itself
Do you ever see a rabbit in it
churning some butter, or

Mindfulness's indifferent, like the wind
That's beautiful, he says thoughtfully
and carefully all falls still in the yard

Thank you, I reply walleyed,
I put it in a romantic poem
I put the moon in most passwords

BRIGHT ANGEL

It's snowing in the Grand Canyon
It's snowing in Central Park in the movies
I miss everything happening all at once
like bopping groundhogs' heads blindfolded
But here we were a married couple sharing
tamales in red sauce and red wine and memories
And vampirically we laughed when we joked
we might push each other into the canyon
as though it were safe as a swimming pool
as though either one of us could swim in the air
Our server said his name was Derrick
and that he'd be our server tonight and
Derrick doesn't care about the view anymore
He said you get used to it after awhile
He said people like to freak out about the elk
And I thought people like to freak out in general
thus Black Friday and horror as an escapism genre
and Elmo and the World Cup and royal weddings
and especially solar eclipses for their rarity
Something to do with adrenaline, spectacle
Not to be confused with real, high-stakes fear
You ordered a brownie and ice cream to go
You left the ice cream outside on the porch
in the cold to keep it cold in the snow

In the Rearview

Lloyd's hogs dissolved

in pale gravel scud.

Mountains rumpled

and shrank like wool.

Impossible horseflies

zagged with conspiracy,

and we agreed: forget it.

Heaviness was felt now

and then, and then

occasionally nothing

but the warm wishes

of our would-be sex cult

toward another open year.

The little edges of the hills

like verdigris knives.

The looping partition,

built to oblige the trees,

rhythmically shifted

below us, silently tectonic,

and the stained glass

mural situation was anything

but mundane. The tesserae,

all fractured reflection,

it was like they knew.

We all knew and felt better

to know we all knew

about the doom, doomed

as it was, as we all were.

It was our doom

and that was all we had,

and in having that

we had mad gladness

as well as other gladnesses

sometimes too. And I tried,

I was trying hard to wag my tail

in time to the warm drone

of slow big band coming nice

and orangely at me like prayer

from another room.

Love Poem Called Die Hard

Tonight you look all menacing and rabid
I want to lick the toothpaste from your chin

Love may be disgusting but the good news is
You'll never kill us both without me, so

I want to put you to sleep but not forever
I want to joust you with a marzipan lance

Shakespeare-style or unlike Bruce Willis
You die hard but you're alive the whole time

Give me *Die Hard* or give me *Mortal Thoughts*
I envy the two tongues of your shoes

You slither into bed with renaissance plasticity
You untuck the duvet of our coeval tomb

It's here I want to remain tonight forever
It's here I could die like an Easter egg

You could crush me like a menthol
With one hand you could drive me

Like the fastest glass motorcycle
Hydroplaning on the river of your blood

The rain falls from a manmade movie rain machine
The rain in Brooklyn falls mainly on the weekends

Here and There

The clouds move in
like quiet neighbors.

The wind
walks down the hill.

The cover crop
has gotten really tall

and I love you.
And the seas are rising

and the meteors
are showering abstractly.

And there are too many guns
and I love you.

I wish I knew what calls
the Devil from the pits —

I have a few theories
scattered though they are

like wildflowers
in the marbleyard.

And I have held a mare
by her matted mane

and clucked my tongue
to summon spring.

And the azaleas
mirror the godlight

and the dogwoods
really do glow in the dark

like the meteors
aforementioned.

I love you
and the horses idle

like old cars
in the shaggy field.

Everyone is poor
but somehow has horses.

I can't explain it
but I wish I could

or how it is a horse is
ever a breakable thing.

STILL TIME ALL DAY

I moved the relief print of the world
to a better place. I covered the trough
to maintain darkness. I am useless!
is what the name of that poem was
that I loved. Any time when I'm alone
I chew my gum and play loud R&B
because there are only so many days
and only almost exactly as many nights.
The leaves are making change, swishily
changing in their chlorophyll dollar bills,
smarter than you or me or dolphins,
even. But there is so much not to know.
How is it that stones hold warmth,
if intermittently alive, like memory?
How is it cymbals have been sounding
since the ancient Armenian Highlands?
Sometimes I send myself dumb letters
like ghosts. They prove like loaves,
like sweaty calculus equations ending
always in the shorthand for treasure.
I used to dig holes in the dark woods
each day thinking this must be the spot.

POEM FOR A FERN

At an outdoor dinner with a hundred friends
at a furniture café called Relationships
someone played celestial harp songs
from their phone over an invisible speaker
and I swear I saw a fern dancing
suspended in a resin wicker basket
from a threshold on the party perimeter
letting down its hundred green hairs

Mama Recites the Birds

I haven't really
taken any notice.

Finches, cardinals,
blue jays, titmouse,
nuthatches, crows,
yellow grosbeaks,

I said titmouse . . .
um, some woodpeckers.
I have sparrows
nesting in the planters . . .

What else:
hawks,
but they don't come to the feeders,
red-tail hawks,

warblers . . .
though I couldn't
tell you what they look like.
You should be calling Becky.

two

BOBBY BORIS PICKETT

For no real good reason
except for the gravity of being alive all the time,

I wept in silence in a corner of the farm.
I climbed the pawpaw tree and shook it hard

and had no bra on and you whistled from below,
waving your hilarious pawpaw stick,

and my wagging boobs waved back hello, hello.
The pawpaws thunked down like library books,

like Brobdingnagian emeralds,
like hours, like rubber hammers,

and passages of light like biblical fragments
stuttered through the evergreen heavens.

And later as the day couldn't last anymore
some nighthawks coolly autographed the dusk,

making their quick crepuscular rounds.
Nothing is the end of the world except climate change,

I reminded the baby in the vanity mirror.
My hand hair turned blonder

and the news moved on without me.
"Monster Mash" at long last loaded on my phone.

It's Sunday so We Get High by the River

The mizuna is up.
The radishes are ready.
Have you seen the spirit yet?
Do you want to check your blood oxygen levels?
The wine delivery deal was a scam, right?
It's a fictional song, a storybook breeze.
A wisp like a lisp through the trees' long limbs.
It's not a measure of your melody but it's fun
to be cutthroat.
We all have our preferred side of the outhouse.
Can I tell you a secret, Charles?
The weedeater mufflers cover wireless headphones perfectly.
A forecast that already happened is a pastcast.

I Went for a Long Ride

My hams pumped and summitted.
Original waters zippered the ridges.
I collected wild chamomile
like chronicles. What else is new?
Everyone wants to know.
The present moment depends on the past

. . . if the past is powerless to interject.
Otherwise known as pigsty daisy.
Alas, more underwear ads.
Locked in a proxy leopard print universe.
Fatigue is a symptom.
So is the moon getting bigger all the while.

Sonnet Near Zyzzyx

We slept sitting up like it was the Middle Ages
in our car in the parking lot at a rest stop in the desert
somewhere near Zyzzyx, California
when all I wanted was to get out of California
and my menstrual cup filled with my chunky blood
and the sun came up like a trend over the faraway rocks
I dreamt a falcon took the diamond from my necklace
and he wouldn't give it back
and you said the symbolism was heavy and obvious
and I thought yeah, like a stone
or a professional wrestler whose ring name says what he does
Big Boss Man, Spanky, Virgil the Kentucky Butcher
The heater had been on high all night heating
My mascara masked my eyes like a racoon

Adidas

You sleep with the fortitude of an eternal winter
You sleep like the dissertation of a blizzard major

You make sleep look like the easiest responsibility
You sleep like a bright white woolen tapestry

You sleep like a garbage truck full of sand
like the very beginning before the beginning began

like the drawing board, like a huddle before a charge
like the mattress is the sprung floor of the sea

Behind your gravity-controlled babydoll eyelids
miniature music like that of a lute reverberates

in an ancient field filled with meaningful stones
and the story in the soil tells us how it was you fell

You fell asleep like a planet falling out of orbit
or heavier, like Pluto falling out of consideration

Or was it that you fell like Niagara or Bridalveil
and did you discover absolute shade at the bottom

You fell well before the well was even cool
when water came only from hot volcanic springs

You sleep like an underachieving simile
You sleep like the first ever baby

You sleep like game over, it was an impossible boss
like you've exhausted every Ninja Turtle in your army

You sleep like the power is out at the feeling factory
Like you came without batteries

You sleep like the power is out for good
and no team of draft horses could turn your bed

Like a high-quality vegetable, maybe kohlrabi
your sleep is the sleep of a secret never spoken aloud

It's like you won the lottery of z's
It's like you drank cement

It's the world's longest underground ellipsis
your dot dot dot suggesting closure by becoming it

Or is it like a pacifistic sovereign nation of dancers
coexisting with a harmony so complex

the effortless elegance of quotidian activities
like doing laundry counts, too, as art

I want to ask permission to dine from your dreams
the good ones like green juice, bad ones like crude oil

like crude oil paintings of dreams yours ooze
beyond form or tradition, that mystery dimension

Like silent film pornography eventually
you come to light with your open mouth vortex

Mouth like the last question ever asked
and forever unanswered

You wake up
like a neon hummingbird

PLAIN AIR
for Andrew Colville

Vulnerability is an open-toed shoe,
a fingerless glove, true love,
a radical re-rendering of the sharing economy.
Madness' house in the middle of all our streets.
Have we discussed this?
The cottonwood seeds quiver into the hall.
The onions become translucent on the stove.
You would think it was a tragic coincidence.
So lambent was your heavy golden chain.
Life is so much shorter than death
in the musty subway hull and in the grand scheme.
Thus once more the sauce gets lost in itself.
I won and all I want to do is go home now.
They should make portals out of poems
so we can be hurt people elsewhere.

Two Pilgrims

Our dirty windows overlook the bay
where people thought they had notions
about the future hundreds of years ago
You sleep through the golden hour

When we argue our vacation away
I want to jump off the Mayflower
or push you off the Mayflower . . .
The water is shallow, cold probably

I try to tell you about a walk I took,
all the rosebushes and the cars I saw
Your summer tan is darker in the dark
You take me out at midnight like a star

This arbitrary holiday weekend
we drift around in our faded sweatshirts
and we reconcile in the dank thicket
where the dunes bury the pines

Things We've Thrown

A lighter
A lint roller
A bag of brown sugar
Knausgaard's *My Struggle,* Book 3
A yellow candle
Our love away
(just kidding)
Some really great parties
A frisbee in an open field
Gummy bears into each other's mouths from all the way across
    the room

Mama Recites the Trees

There are so many!
Of course I don't know how many species of oaks
but there are a lot of native oaks:

willow oak
red oak
white oak
black oak?
It's possible
I don't think they're super common

Willow oaks like swampy areas
so down near the river
where you see the smaller trees
some of them still have tree tubes
some of those are willow oaks because they like to be wet

We do have some red maples here but they're not as common
Sugar maples are more common
Red maples give that brilliant color

And there are locust trees
and you know
so many different varieties

You have your evergreen trees

We pretty much wiped out the paradise trees at Claytor
which are invasive
they send up saplings from the roots and they're difficult to kill

You have to wait for summer when it's really horrible outside
and every summer I follow the trees with an axe
and I squirt a poison into the hackmarks
Yep

What it did was . . . the tree was waning
so the sap was starting to go down to the root system
Paradise trees don't have seed pods

End of July end of August
we're tromping through the forest in the fucking heat
We call it hack and squirt

Hack and squirt!
We're murderers

When Dan retires
I'm gonna dig up a sapling and pot it for him
Hahaha

He's also on the bittersweet trail
which is also invasive

He's gotten most of it but they have these little red berries
that the birds will carry and drop and spread
It's gonna be someone else's lifelong pleasure

Kinda like kudzu
we're borderline with kudzu
we keep it contained
we can't kill all of it

There's dogwoods
and redbuds!

Oh my favorite, cedar trees!
Hahaha

Cedar trees are okay once they get mature
but they're a nuisance to me, which you know!
You'll never let me live that one down

They're bushy, prickly, ugly, I don't know
they kind of brown up in the winter

They are good trees for birds to nest in
because they're so thick snakes don't want to climb up in them to
    snag their eggs
I'm just not fond of cedar trees, never have been
I do like the smell
and the wood is lovely, it really is
so it does have its qualities

even though I found out that cedar chests . . . okay,

the oil in cedar trees never stops
it's considered kind of a soft wood
even when you go to the core of the tree where it's red and harder
people use
the oil deteriorates the thread!
So the best thing to do is put them in plastic and then put them in a
    cedar chest
and then they're okay

Dan is like tree guy

I used to be able to really identify trees when I was a little girl

It was Warren Henegar who taught me identification
He was a conservation officer
and that's what I wanted to be when I was little
I wanted to be like Warren
I wanted to marry him
I was Warren's special little Liell girl

In Indiana, all fifth grade students spend one week at
    a state park camp

I wasn't very popular

Oh my god
Okay

white pine
cedars
oaks
maples
locusts
buh buh buh . . . You're catching me at a bad time of night
dogwood
redbud
blackhaw, which is interesting
sassafras

It's late for Mommy

birch
beech trees
tulip poplars

There's one at the corner of the front of the house that has grown
    so much
and I love it because it's just this nice tall tree

Dan's favorite tree is a tulip poplar! And I was amazed by that

magnolia
sweetgum

I mean we have a really amazing diversity of trees around here

Miracle-Gro

Gloria instructs me to protect the climbing vine
best I can from the blackberry bush

And my arms tear open like junk mail
from the thorns and I do feel closer to Jesus

however miniscule my suffering by comparison
and small the central sliver of our Venn diagram otherwise

A valiant effort is made in the garden
And later a box of new socks and old pears appears in the cabin

among other goodies from over the mountain
the pears from Argentina

sweet in that distinctively milky pear way
freckled from their marathon voyage

You wonder if there exists a pear without freckles
If freckles are punctuation marks in the paragraph of the face

If freckles were among the smallest shrapnel
expelled in the glossy dawn of the universe

What a time to be alive
I wonder unironically aloud to no one

three

CAREER

I spent all my avocado money
by the light of Saint Martin de Porres
I often think about bank robbery
what wig I would wear, what fun it would be
to harm no one and dump a million dollars
over the hills that belong to everyone
from an airplane that I teach myself to fly

SOME SUNLIGHT

Loneliness prances by like an invisible bull
where I loll at the overgrown rodeo.
You would've loved it.
I dribbled orange juice all over the bleachers.
I peed in the weeds.
I sat there for hours and hours with a giant book
I didn't read.
A gate rattled against itself in the distance.
Existence, existence.
"Incalculable Loss," says the *Times*.
The warmth of some sunlight on my back.
The pizzicato footsteps of a quail in the grass.

Beautiful Daggers

The ides come and go as lovers
exercise in afternoon's cool limit.
The moon like a spot of drool
on the sky's baby blue baby bib.
Snow frowns back into the ground.
Crocuses occur from nothing and
miracle out in their satin purpleness.
Taxes, shmaxes. Caesar swoons
and the robins remember, cheerio.
The cotyledon tip their little hats,
my green friends, my future flowers.
I guess I haven't yet opened up
the salsa or the pregnancy tests.
But there is so much else to do.
The man who makes windows
works on the house across the way
all day. Bobcats live their wild lives
somewhere far up in the mountain.

Homecoming Pain

Bring back the woolly mammoth
and the silky mammoth and the sequin mammoth.
Bring back fringe. Bring back profiteroles.
Bring it on back. Please just take it on home.
Send us back before we were ever here,
ever etched here into the trunk of a tree.
Before a person could ever do any harm.
Take it down a notch. Take it slow
and go back, back, back to the pre-dawn past.
Bring back my Bonnie to me and my mammoth.
Bring back the floppy disc and keep only one copy
burnt image of a memory of my mammoth and me.
Mommy and mammoth and me. Nature!
Where the chef works for no man, for no money.

Sweet Pea

We have sweet pea —
anarchical accomplices,
may we rest well for once.
We've had some good rain,
this wine was free,
and my old mutt is still alive
as this poem is written.
May Jackson be forever
immortalized in this poem.
Look how he stirs in the shade.
Look at those twitchy, tawny ears.
There is such a thing as a good boy
and Jackson is the example.
Hear the noiseless applause
of his eyelashes open and close
as clouds collide overhead
and spill together like curtains
or like old cereal milk.
Who doesn't love spring,
pointing toward eternity
its long, blossoming branch?
It's like pressing the backs of
your hands against a door frame
from within the door frame
and holding them there
and counting to sixty
and then letting go
and floating away

Jenny Talking about Twilight Knowing

I get it
I think I get it

Everyone is happy and so am I
The juneberry era, the dogwood time

Do you ever wake up smiling?
(really though)

The doe bounds through the high glittering wheat
of wet daybreak

The steam puffs up off the pond
back up into the air

to be air again
Back home again

The morning creatures
say Here now, here now

and Ah ah ah ah
It's so fucking beautiful

sometimes
if I may say so

The liminal space
the vague hither thither

The tadpoles' eloquent
s's in the water

FUTURE BROOCHES

There is a dangerous beach outside of Big Lagoon
with a steep shelf where the waves come up like walls
and crash like walls. And one evening,
approaching nautical twilight, I saw some people
hunched over in the sand. Their body language told me
they were studying something, but what it was was unclear.
I figured this was one of those moments I would never know
    the answer
unless I were to ask. The waves crashed and crashed.
So I approached some of these crouching people, of which
there were several, and asked what it was they were looking for
and could I help? If they needed any help?
It felt like showing up to dress rehearse a pivotal scene
in a play whose script I had practiced in the car
and poorly. I wasn't sure what it was I was prepared to offer
given my limited skill set of, I don't know, making bûche de Noël,
whatever else it is I do. And the sand people said, Looking for agate,
and I said What? Agate! They said, their fingers like spiders.
Oh, I said, like I understood. And then one day I did.

Late Spring Poem

after Ian Munn

I try to be honest on the long questionnaire.
The lights are white. My skin is cold

in the air conditioning. The PHQ-9
asks if I have had little interest or pleasure

in doing things, on a scale of not at all
to several days to more than half the days

to nearly every day, over the last two weeks.
I love to see the word *pleasure* there.

At Goodwill I find a purple skirt with little flowers
and Mariah Carey's Greatest Hits on CD

and two worn Rand McNally children's books,
one called *Let's Grow Things* about gardens and

one called *The Little Mailman of Bayberry Lane*,
basically about friendship. The Little Mailman

of Bayberry Lane is a little chipmunk
who's well loved by the neighborhood

and he's super sociable and kind and whistling
all the time and pretty much everyone gets mail

every day in this order: Mrs. Goose,
Mrs. Duck, Mr. Turtle, and Mrs. Pig.

And Mrs. Goose always makes bayberry candles
and she wears a red bandana with little white flowers

and Mrs. Duck sweeps the yellow leaves off her walk
and she always hopes there's a letter from her sister

and she wears a checkered apron and holds her broom
and looks forlornly down the lane.

And Mr. Turtle sits on his front stairs in the sun,
eyes closed, wearing a little white and green hat,

wondering if today's the day the tulip catalog comes,
but he's not particularly impatient or anything.

And Mrs. Pig wears a white dress that ties in the back
with little pink flowers and she has a special day

when she bakes something special, which is
Friday, so this Friday she makes apple tarts

which the Little Mailman enjoys very much
and tells Mrs. Pig she's the best and so on,

and anyway the Little Mailman goes home
to his house under the stone wall and reflects

on his day and why Mrs. Pig never gets any mail,
because she doesn't, and he thinks, Oh,

you know, she must not write any letters,
oh because she must not have any friends,

and why doesn't she have any friends,
and why doesn't she go out and make some,

and yeah, maybe she feels socially awkward
or maybe prefers the perfect relative privacy

of her quiet, introverted life to herself
and well, she is a really great baker and all,

and the Little Mailman sits at his adorable table
with his tiny quill pen under the soft warm flame

of one of Mrs. Goose's bayberry candles
and he writes invitations to all the neighbors

for a surprise party he wants to throw Mrs. Pig.
And he plans it for the following Friday

because he can count on Mrs. Pig to bake
something special like she would already do

and she wouldn't know about the surprise
because she never receives any mail, so

she wouldn't think it was strange not to
get an invitation. Right, and everyone conspires

and everyone gets ready for the big party
and Mrs. Goose irons her party sash

and Mrs. Duck adorns herself with extra feathers
and Mr. Turtle shakes out the mothballs

from the pockets of his party jacket.
And Mrs. Pig doesn't know any of this

and she lonesomely shuffles around at home
wearing the same dress and making apple tarts

again but this time also little lemon cakes
dotted with hickory nuts which sounds great

and she goes outside while the cakes cool
and she's picking chrysanthemums by the stone wall

when surprise! Everyone jumps out
with their respective plus-ones, it's a big party,

except Mr. Turtle who seems to have come alone
and he's wearing a cute little brown bowler hat

and he gives Mrs. Pig a special tulip bulb
and Mrs. Goose has brought a bayberry candle

and Mrs. Duck has brought a feather duster
and the Little Mailman brings a whole basket

of hickory nuts and we are told
It was the happiest afternoon of Mrs. Pig's life,

and they all play croquet and stay up late
and the next day Mrs. Pig gets six letters in the mail

which is really exciting and sweet because
they're all thank you letters from the party guests

thanking Mrs. Pig for such a great party
and she stands there and reads them at the mailbox.

And the Little Mailman is out on his route somewhere,
swinging his satchel of envelopes and whistling

and it's so nice because I too like to whistle
and I too like to wait for the tulip catalog

and friendships are pretty fucking awesome
even in these fucked up, sad centuries

and on the drive home from free therapy
I listen to "Heartbreaker" with the windows down

which thwacks my hair all over the place
which I kind of love because I don't care

and the sky is big and bright and June-y blue
and there are all the little flowers in the world.

Leaving the House

Leaving the house
like salad
usually requires dressing

four

SUMMER OF THE WILD BOARS

You looked good in those all-purpose sneakers
but what of mambo numbers one through four?
They rescued the soccer team from the cave

I heard the news on public radio
as the sun got in the car
gingerly through the sunroof

The Long Blue Dress

I whooshed
through the party.

I grew
a set of invisible hands.

I was flower girl
to the Commonwealth

where lovers danced a dance
called the snowdrift.

Sugar maples
helicoptered

samaras
in my glass.

The dogs slackened
in their webs of shade.

A democracy
of clouds formed,

a storm
was decided.

Everyone inside,
candles on.

I say
it makes sense!

Every raindrop
a little bell,

every switchback
and holler baptized.

But it felt
so good to cry.

I stacked
the wood so high

I never again left.
I never again wore shoes.

My long blue dress
suggested my power,

my powerful sadness.
And you and you

and you
and the gyrating populace

and everyone
was there.

Mama Sows the Ginseng Seeds

On the other side of the new creek
above bottle dump first plot between
rocks and cut walnut tree on the
fence line next other side of downed
tree base of poplar fourth plot near
under grape vine fifth plot upstream
across from old hunting stand past
double grape vine under poplar with
one grape vine locust behind it next
plot twenty feet above near fence
between double trunk tree and small
stones two on top of a larger one
twelve feet up next to fence next
one ten feet up planted five for the
sun stopped at rocks old stump with
wire next down and past old stump
planted five cross over walnut tree
planted in front of broken egg rock
day two lower field cross stream
and upstream just a bit from beech
tree field side in front of smaller
beech tree next across from bottom
field on fence line near downed pine
planted beside ironwood tree further
down on fence row in front of old
metal bucket past downed ash tree
in front and beside cedars way down
on the other side of the old creek

Romance Language

It's the endangered language of endangered birds.

High notes neglected by textbook indexes, low notes too.

It's a whoop and a coo and the trilling of a trumpet all at once.

It's the sound of the ocean waving its infinite wet handkerchiefs
    goodbye, goodbye . . .

It's all the tears the sky has ever cried.

It's the language between one bell and another bell as they chime
    the same song.

You can hear the ding of the brass pass across the mossy
    quadrangle . . .

It's written only in ribbons of lemon and orange peel curls.

It's Jimmy Mack's explanation for disappearing in the first place.

It's writ in glass rejectamenta down at Dead Horse Bay.

You can piece it back together if you have a thousand odd years.

The instructions are written in . . . this language.

It's the language of many-teethed sunflowers' midsummer chatter.

It's the language of babbling, dribbling, blubbering, shrubbery, and
    bubblegum.

Hobby linguists found this language in cubbyhole rubble.

It's the language of chauffeurs' idling cars' doors ajar.

It's the mirage that blurs and lifts up off the tar.

It's the slow opening of chiffonier and credenza drawers . . .

It's the shimmying walls of a canyon refracting an echo of the words *echo* and *I love you, I love you.*

It's the language of mothers and of motherfuckers and it has no gender.

It sounds like it's important, and it is . . .

It's the language of the historical future, after all.

It rolls off the tongue and lands in the mossy quadrangle of the past.

It's a time-traveling language that will outlive the mouth.

It rolls off the tongue into traffic and survives.

It's a limited edition addition made different, different again.

It's different from coincidence, but eerily similar . . .

It's the rare phenomenon of double jinx. / It's the rare phenomenon of double jinx.

It's the secret ingredient in a good aurora borealis but shh.

It rolls off the tongue and back up the tongue and you can swallow it whole.

You can swallow it like a vitamin, or a pearl, or pride.

You can pick it up simply by listening. (*I love you . . .*)

You can pick it up with your bare hands, but understand that this language is heavy.

It's the language the seashell itself hears.

It's the language of rustling bushes, hushes, crushes . . .

It's the language bad boys teach you after curfew in the park.

As with any other language, learn the curse words first.

You can learn it on a long drive or on a slow train.

It's the language of living, giving, and forgiving things.

You can learn it in the last wing of a large museum.

It's the wind in winter woods like *whew* . . . (*I love you* . . .)

It's the rains that finally arrive, writhing down the mountainside.

Your face flushes when you speak it. You can't help it . . .

It ushers new eras. It tickles the ears.

It's a green mound. It's a mondegreen.

It flies from the diaphragm lean with ambition.

Sonnet for a Good Cry in the Woods

Love is a babe, pig in the city.
Like that scene in *Amour*
where, well, they smother each other.
Everyone agrees it's kind of beautiful.
Another motorbike zooms wizardly by
the tulips like interrobangs on Park Avenue.
Meanwhile I'm sorry I'm so sad, meanwhile
everyone else is busy moving to Asheville.
The earnest shame of writing poetry
while my friends manually labor!
But I, too, have woke for the worms,
I have eaten weeds, for the record.
Take my picture with this bag of chips.
Quick, I'll never be this young again.

Nightgown

You made us lunch
I tried on bygone clothes
then tried them off

I went through a phase
where I wore negligees
in daytime as dresses

I loved the appliqués
embroidered roses
the luster of the tulle

I folded
one white silk number
I've never worn

I sleepwalked
to the kitchen
I stirred the macaroni

I HAVE YET MORE ESOTERICISM TO SHARE

At the Santa Cruz Public Storage
sharing a too-hard persimmon
I hate what we've gone through
but I love that we've gone through it

But where was all the wildlife?
Why is the werewolf shirtless all the time?*
When danger takes you by the ankles
you slip out of your socks like *aha*

*we all know why

True Life:

I disappear
in a tendril of cerulean
storm drain steam.

I reappear
the next season
as myself.

five

Grimaldo's Chair

Champagne brained, ocean haired
I bike my way home in a merciful drizzle

and the birds are waking each other up
as though today, too, is important. I realize

my closest friends are the ones I never speak to
like we're mimes on the same side of a silent war.

I write this down in the wet sand of my memory
I shake out the sand from my shoes when I'm home,

waiting for my toast to toast . . . I guess
I'm still pretty giddy when I bike to work

over the bridge over the river and into the city
for another slow shift at the pajama store.

Hannah leaves for Paris for the summer the same day
the president changes his mind about the airstrike.

THE LITTLE NEWS

I'm in my shed watching *Captain America*
hitting the one-hitter for the sixth time, so, twice thrice
A courteous rain neatly garnishes the roof and
I am less like surrounded by the sounds of popping corn
(as the tin roof usually simulates when it rains) and more like
someone is gently clicking their fingernails against my skull
like they are making a thinking motion for me or like
the motion I would make if I told you I was reading your mind
but we were standing too far away from one another
to say it aloud so motion was all we could rely on
and maybe a really smooth song was a scrim in the room
and people were making out and laughing and bragging all
around us stories like little ladders we use to teeter over
the hedges of what comes next in our social thoughts
I love to read your mind
When asked if I have a favorite book
I want to say your mind, of course
Four
Ladybug
Wholesome
Saltines

HE LOVES ME

He loves me not.
But there's a sexy glitch in the matrix
that lets you walk through walls.
There's a whole lot of roses
in the rosebushes by the gas station
like what is this, a fragrance commercial?
A church burns down in the village.
I can see the smoke from up on the bridge
remembering to breathe both ways.
My lungs like a frayed denim butterfly
shaggily pulsing all through summer.
Outside is still, with some conditions, free.
Most nights I want to run out in the street,
animal in my scandalous bedroom britches.
I don't want to miss the sun's finale,
its orange monologue, its red aside, its sigh
as it slips into the dark robe of nothingness . . . again.
Look at that bad boy locking, popping, dropping,
says Pat, it doesn't seem so far away after all.
Some birds land on and lift off of the river
without stopping the flapping of their wings.
He loves me.

The Fleece

Alone in bed
I'm waiting for another
mean green storm.

Cassini crashes into Saturn
and suddenly I'm older
than I ever was before.

Sacerdotal hollandaise.
Auspicious precipitation. See,
there are words for all this.

So we changed
the nature of how
we articulate landscape.

The river is silver.
The ride is treacherous.
An angel gifs its wings.

You come to bed.
The air of wet cement
and smoke becomes you.

You unfold
the fleece
like a big love letter.

Really I'm dying
but in an opposite way.
I'm going to seed.

I'm shooting up a flower
like a little yellow flare
. . . so there.

Just as there is truth
in every joke there is truth
in a double dog dare.

The effort.
The Eiffel Tower.
The two quartz threads.

I am trying
to describe cosmic rays
to you here.

How implacable
the crackle of light is
when it strikes you.

POEM FOR A FIELDMOUSE

Every night the cats catch a mouse
I rescue the mouse in a yogurt container
and take it outside and let it go.
Every night for as long as I can remember
or at least as many make a pattern,
I rescue these mice and it's a wonder
I have so many yogurt containers
and that the cats never seem to understand
what's happening. I set the little guy down
by the woodpile tonight. He'll have the option
to seek out the shallots in the shed if he wants
or maybe find his family, I project sentimentally.
He didn't seem hurt so much as he seemed alarmed
and, you know, he looked sort of familiar.
Either I'm rescuing the same mouse every night
or he can't believe his own freedom either,
or both, lord help us, both things are true.

My Neighbor Says His Friend Says

If you drink too much blue Gatorade you die.
I say wow, do you think that's true?
and he shrugs and says he likes the reds and oranges.
His little brother gives me a dried pear from a brown paper bag.

Then they run back down the road to their house.
Then the planet keeps spinning on its spindly tilted axis
and the next day when they're done with Zoom school
they give me a painting of a dragon with two mouths.

I say wow, I see the two mouths!
And we sit outside and watch the butterflies flitter and
just as I'd begun to mourn certainty itself, the little brother says,
Those aren't butterflies, they're cabbage moths.

Mama Recites the Horses

I do remember
I can rattle them off

So there is . . . okay I'm starting from the beginning to the end

Deedee and Tory
who were the last ones here

Eddie who threw me numerous times
Threw me like three times

He was the one that got ruptured in his penis by Sam the pony

So Sam the pony and Liz
are buried here
in the very bottom below the patio

At Doug and Cathy's there was Flint
the little black horse

Trying to think
Steve rode Liz? I rode . . .

Flint was the black horse that was Cathy's

Then for a short time

We got Dances off of a trailer
coming from Alabama
and she was a beautiful palomino
beautiful white mane, really pretty

and she was crazy 'cause they drugged her
and Margie's dogs chased her through the fence
and she cut her leg really bad
and I got Emile's wife Karen to come and look at her
and she was like Oh you just take a garden hose

They were buying donkeys from Doug and Cathy
and somehow on the internet somehow some way
we bought Dances

And then we had another horse
who was buckskin with black mane and tail
one of the prettiest horses I've ever seen
and your stepsister Margaret tried to put a hat on her
and she bucked, like pawed at her

she was a beautiful horse but she was fucking crazy
and she went to a meatpacking place

All horses who are processed for dog meat or whatever
go to Canada now
because Americans love their horses
they don't want them in the dog food

Nelly!

Nelly was at Doug and Cathy's
so it was

Nelly
Liz
the horse that kept throwing me
Eddie

and Sam the pony
and Rusty the pony

and guess who's still alive!
Star the fucking donkey is still alive

and he gets out all the time
I see him on the side of the road
fat as he is tall

Colie
Yep, the white draft horse
she was a sweetheart

We ended up cutting a big oak tree at the ridge line
looking down from the house
and Steve cut the tree just at the right height

Colie was just tall enough
you could see her
she would go across the stump like she was humping it
but she'd be scratching her belly
scratching her belly

I was just thinking of Deedee and Tory

She's okay

I think she's doing okay

They're not riding her a whole lot
because she's founded
it's when you eat too much and the enzymes go to their hoofs

They're on the other side of Bedford
Moneta basically

beautiful view

Deedee has a better view there
than she did here

She's well taken care of
I do feel good about that

Alone Time

How to tell of the cherry tree
in spring but with piano.

There's no knowing,
only the miracle of flight,

a periwinkle winged thing
I first saw as a flower.

I am at my most at home
at home. The illusion of how

the clouds around the mountains
make the mountains look bigger —

is there anything lovelier than rain
and the day once the rain is done?

Having a bath,
I traipse around the lower field,

pines soft as girlfriends,
grasses' nonsense promises

whispers against my ankles'
naked white knobs, so

secondhand and loose
in my corduroy coveralls.

It can be a frightening thing
to find yourself, but isn't it

still worse to lose
yourself altogether?

Or is it,
or is it?

I find the spine and skull
of a deer not long ago

gone, and I take some
to give to the dogs.

Dully clattering
through the holler,

why is it I am
always bringing home bones —

Sonnet from Last July

The droughted leather hills rolled toward the bay.
We split fog with our great machine. More sun shone.
We bought pluots, blue cheese, cheap riesling, and
I wanted to fuck, marry, and kill you all at once.
We went with the first two things, which was nice.
I said, That was nice, when you made me cum.
I came as a car alarm sounded. I came as four flies
peppered the hot dry air of our friends' living room.
I wanted to tell you my worst ideas about the plot
for my best idea about the novel as your heart slowed
in our tranquil anticlimax. Honey dozed in the bamboo.
Tinny reggae thrummed vaguely behind the hedgerow.
The redwood roots busted up through the pavement
like the veins on the backs of both our tired hands.

six

Drama Club

It's kind of nice
no one cares I'm writing poetry

Everyone's secrets
safe with me

Eating yesterday's noodles
wearing my favorite brown socks

I talk to my cousin
I talk to my brother

I try to call my sister
but she's feeding the cows

cinnamon raisin bread
out in the cold

At least everyone is talking
to each other and not afraid to cry

A thousand years have passed
just today

ANOTHER SUNDAY POEM

Cancel rent

We're out at the sunset again
above the tubs
below big birds
cliff types   hugging

cypresses like creepy green gloves
(creepy in a beautiful way)

You said a canyon
is an inverted mountain

I was thinking
god you're smart

When I pass back the spliff on the park bench
I just don't want any children to see me
setting bad examples everywhere I go . . .

We're trying to spell the woman's name
who lives in the valley with one long grey braid

We need a place with a yard
We need to show our friends the same
hospitality they have shown us for millennia

A language that adequately confronts
the flaws that keep us from becoming
the country we could be

In other words, the truth is
truth cannot be conflated with beauty
when beauty is an empty idea

Like a jpeg
of a painting

Land's End is
full of people today
little blankets
plates of food

Couples kissing
behind jagged rocks

Couples kissing
on the edge of history

Taking subtly different pictures
of the same regular phenomenon

(the sun)
    (setting)

How is it
this happens all the time

THE BIRDS DID IT

O wild bushes wobbling in the wind!
O evening sun!
I am a little drunk
and finally at ease
having walked through Spain.

O sunflower! Sunflower, twinkle
your seeds all over me and
bury me alive in light.
Next year I'll reemerge
and they'll say the birds did it.

AIMLESSNESS

I bike out to the park every day in September
trying to remember the third doorway to wisdom.

    1. I am not myself,
    2. nothing lasts
        (which is huge load off),
    3. and . . .

These geese give me a look
like they could kill me if they wanted
and you know what, I don't blame them.
I would kill myself too if — no, I won't joke about that.

I flash a peace sign to the man in the gazebo.
He nods like he holds a copy of the key.

SONNET FOR YOUR SOILS

We're outside and you're showing me your soils
and your mulches and your mycorrhizae and your buckets.
For the life of me I'm trying to recite Keats'
"When I have fears that I may cease to be"
but I'm too messed up after dinner to get the end right.
You say it's pretty good, though.
Our dahlias are drying on twine in the corner
of the dimly lit lean-to area by the carport.
It'll be full-on autumn soon, my nipples always know.
That's a pretty good trick, you say suggestively.
Never have relish in the faery power
Of unreflecting love — then I get the rest
but the last line always irks me.
What are you writing? you ask. Secrets, I tell you.

This Is Also That

The sun is a pumpkin.
The pumpkin is a small sun.
The pumpkin is a small hard sun.
The pumpkin is fun. Orange
is fun and the hard orange sun
is a small fun orange pumpkin.
The orange pumpkin is in the fall.
The fall of the orange sun is small.
The hard orange fall is fun and
the orange is in the feather.
The sun is the hard orange feather.
The fun feather is the small spirit.
The orange spirit is the twist
and the twist is the small fun fall.
The twist is the twist is the dance.

Mama Recites the Plot of a Liam Neeson Movie Called Honest Thief

It's Liam Neeson
he's a good thief
he's a bank robber

He was a marine
with PTSD from his dad who got laid off and lost his pension
His dad killed himself because he lost his pension

Then he wants to get back at the system
He's a special military bomb expert so he can blow up vaults and shit
Then he robs banks for like two years

Then he turns into the good thief
and decides to take the money he has in the storage unit of the
    woman he falls in love with
He tries to turn himself in and the FBI agents take the money

After Hours

I'm in a graveyard
in Vermont in 2021
identifying fox-and-cubs

or orange hawkweed
or orange hawkbit
or devil's paintbrush

or grim-the-collier,
thinking about love again
and lots of other things.

Earlier this morning
I met some folks who live
in a house attached to a train,

and later tonight
I'll finally wash my hair.
And how love is

especially strange.
The graveyard is
so green right now

and soft underfoot
and full of the breath
that we know as wind

from all the souls.
As usual, I have no idea
what it is I'm doing

but anyway, here we are.
We just give it away,
that's what we do with it

when we don't know
what to do with it.
Before me, a daddy long legs

goes running, running,
running, running,
running, running,

running, running,
all those eight feet at once.
The image of grace,

I want to say,
but what I mean is *an* image
of grace, just one of

many images there are
in the world. Little daddy
long legs, so small

and faint and full
of grace, goes through
the grass like a memory

and then I lose track of it.
And when we do know,
we give sometimes

with great purpose.
I really believe in that,
purpose — the poignancy

of this careening
through life and all.
It is so green here,

I am reminded of kissing
and quitting my job
and also of wasabi.

The sky,
with a little pink in it,
like forgotten citrus

or tourmaline
or the feeling of swimming
or horniness.

These beautiful gravestones
don't care, or maybe they do.
I never remember what it is

I'm getting at
except that it's further
from where it was I started.

LIVEPOWER, OR, BIODYNAMISM

That small thunder thunders as I enter the barn
As the steer's legs fold beneath him like a card

His open eyes like out of order crystal balls
Like he was in the middle of delivering prophecy

Blood sneaks under the hay to the floor of the manger
That place of divine birth and of modest death

There's incarnation and then there's excarnation,
Stephen says, and that's just how it all goes

Thank you for helping me wash my hands
Thank you for lunch and the little bowl hit

And for going down on me despite everything
As if one of these days will really be the end

BENEDICTION

Long live
the short shelf life
of the sunset.

Bless
the cedar waxwing
in the juniper bush.

Celebrate
the lightning bugs'
cyberpunk semaphore.

Praise
the muskmelons'
fulgid orange insides.

Revere
the toads, the slugs,
the turtles, the skunks.

Admire
the rattlesnake shaking
the beans of its maraca.

Give thanks
to the chickens
for giving us eggs.

Laud
the basil
and the holy basil.

Behold
the porcelain doorknob
of the buck moon.

Godspeed
the baby bunnies
in the driveway.

Resolutions

Read more
Write more
More walks
Lots more bike
Less phone
More friends
Read *Ulysses*
More soups and
more good butter
Be like an otter
in the water
Be like water
supple-strong
melodious
not always blue

Notes

"Here and There" reckons with a line from an amazing Ruth Stone poem called "The Season."

The poem referred to in "Still Time All Day" is "I Am Useless" by Alfonsina Storni. It really is such a great poem.

"Poem for a Fern" is for Relationships. For Hannah, for Austin. For Su and Nina.

"I Have Yet More Esotericism to Share" borrows its title from . . . somewhere??

"Sonnet Near Zyzzyx" should spell "Zyzzyx" as "Zzyzx," but it does not.

"Plain Air" is for Andrew Colville. He is loved and missed.

The title "Jenny Talking About Twilight Knowing" was scribbled down while listening to Jenny Offill talk about "twilight knowing" in an interview, a concept elaborated upon in her brilliant book *Weather*. The line "Everyone is happy and so am I" is a riff on a line from Malcolm Lowry's *Under the Volcano*.

"Late Spring Poem" makes reference to the Patient Health Question-naire, a self-administered depression survey developed by medical professionals at Columbia University with a grant from Pfizer in the mid-to-late 1990s. "Late Spring Poem" also borrows a line from (and draws from the plot of) *The Little Mailman of Bayberry Lane*, written by Ian Munn, illustrated by Elizabeth Webbe, published by Rand McNally in 1952.

"Sonnet for a Good Cry in the Woods" doesn't exactly or accurately capture what happens in the movie *Amour* (no spoilers), but it is a great movie, and so is *Babe*. "Love is a babe" comes from Shake-speare's Sonnet CXV: *Love is a babe; then might I not say so, / To give full growth to that which still doth grow?*

"Grimaldo's Chair" is for all my quiet friendships.

"My Neighbor Says His Friend Says" is for Rufus and Jules.

"Alone Time" makes reference to the very beautiful song "Having a Bath" by h hunt.

"Sonnet for Your Soils" makes a mess of Keats' "When I Have Fears That I May Cease to Be."

"This Is Also That" is reminiscent of a Mark Leidner poem called "Lily Pad," which I love (*and love is rad*).

"After Hours" borrows a line from a Frank O'Hara prose poem called "Birdie."

"Livepower, or, Biodynamism" is for Stephen Decater.

"Resolutions" reflects a piece of advice from my cousin Elliott.

Acknowledgments

Thank you forever to the editors of the following journals for first publishing versions of some of these poems. Thank you for your time, your generosity of mind, your excellent taste (haha), and your guidance.

The American Poetry Review: "Career" and "Bright Angel"
Bennington Review: "The Fleece"
The Boiler Journal: "Sonnet Near Zyzzyx" and "I Have Yet More Esotericism to Share"
b l u s h: "Poem for a Fern" and "Sonnet for a Good Cry in the Woods"
CutBank: "Poem for a Fieldmouse"
The Greensboro Review: "Some Sunlight"
Guesthouse: "Future Brooches"
Mikrokosmos: "Grimaldo's Chair"
The Oakland Review: "Love Poem Called Die Hard"
Pouch: "Nature Documentary" and "Nightgown"
Sixth Finch: "The Big Egg" and "Adidas"
Southwest Review: "Romance Language"
Raleigh Review: "My Neighbor Says His Friend Says"
SAND: "Homecoming Pain"
Voicemail Poems: "Mama Recites the Birds"

There are so many folks to thank for . . . everything. I swear I tried to make this shorter!

The earliest poems to take root in this book came from my time in the CUNY Brooklyn College MFA program, where I had the unreal honor of studying with Julie Agoos, Anselm Berrigan, Elaine Brooks, Ben Lerner, Marjorie Welish, and Mac Wellman. Thank you all. Thank you to my MFA cohort, whose poems and visions helped shape my own poems and visions by the haunted glow of Dante's bust: Melanie Best, Laura Catella Georgi, Rami Karim, Leah Kiureghian, Raffi

Kiureghian, Zach LaMalfa, Mike Samra, and Jennifer Stella. Thanks to Ellen Tremper, Bonnie Harris, and everyone at BC. Thank you to my students — *you* taught *me*, after all. And thanks to the Truman Capote Literary Trust for awarding me a fellowship, without which graduate school may not have seemed possible.

Thank you to every single educator, from public school to Bennington, who has ever shaken my brain up and down like a bag of so many frozen peas.

To the crew that keeps the Claytor Nature Center quite literally alive: Dan, Greg, Trish, and even Thomas, if you're reading this. Thank you strong, wonderful people.

Thank you to Andrew Barton for printing and championing *Country Music*, the chapbook where a handful of these poems first fell into conversation with one another. Hell yes, Two Plum Press. And thank you to Stacy Skolnik and Katie Della-Valle and everyone at Montez Press for making *Mummy* happen. Special warmth always to Daisy Parris.

Extra loving thanks to my friend Farhad Mirza. To what's next.

Thank you to Nate Luce for lending "Giovanna" as *Bright Shade's* easy breezy beautiful covergirl. Cheersing you with your own aquavit.

Infinite thanks to Elizabeth Scanlon — for your positivity, your patience, your support, your devotion to this thing called poetry, and everything that you do. You make this real, you know. Thanks also, big time, to The American Poetry Review, the Honickman Foundation, and Copper Canyon Press. I am a lucky, lucky duck.

Turns out the APR / Honickman legacy is full of angels disguised as poets, and they walk amongst us on Earth. To Taneum Bambrick, Tomás Q. Morín, Chessy Normile, and Natasha Rao, thank you for being so ridiculously lovely (and smart, and cool, and blah blah blah). xxoo

Thank you, Jericho Brown. Thank you for seeing something in these crazy poems, and what's more, for believing in them. Thank you for advising me to make this the book I wanted to be a book. Thank you for your granular attention, your intuition, your words. Thank you for taking me and my work seriously and yet with levity, with total kindness, with heart. Thank you.

Rivers of thanks and love to my family, both given and chosen. Thank you, friends. Thank you, creatures great and small.

Thank you, circumferentially, to Harrison. Amore et melle et felle est fecundissimus. I love you, I do.

And thank you, of course, to my one and only Mama, my Maggy, my mom. None of us are long for this world.